The Art of Leadership: Navigating the Path to Success

Thank you,
I cannot express enough gratitude for your purchase of my book. Your support means everything and I'm truly humbled that you have chosen to invest your time and resources into reading my work. It fills me with a sense of purpose to know that my words have reached you. Thank you for being a part of my journey and for supporting my passion. I hope that you find value in my words and that they help further excel you towards your goals and dreams.

With sincere appreciation,
Ronald Bizzle

The Art of Leadership: Navigating the Path to Success

1. **Introduction**..3
   - Definition of leadership..4
   - Importance of leadership in various fields..................6
   - Purpose of the book 8
2. **The Traits of Effective Leaders**...............................10
   - Characteristics and qualities of effective leaders..........11
   - Developing the Traits of Effective Leaders. 14
   - Examples of Leaders Who Possess the Traits of Effective Leaders...17
3. **The Different Styles of Leadership**.........................20
   - Overview of the various leadership styles..................21
   - Advantages and disadvantages of each style.............24
   - How to determine the best leadership style for a given situation..27
4. **Leading Teams and Organizations**.........................29
   - The role of the leader in building and leading teams...30
   - How to create a positive and productive work environment...32
   - Strategies for effective communication and delegation...35
5. **Managing Change and Conflict**..............................38
   - The leader's role in managing change and conflict......39
   - Strategies for effectively navigating resistance to change..41
   - Techniques for resolving conflicts and promoting collaboration..43
6. **Developing and Mentoring Others**.........................45
   - The importance of developing and mentoring others..46
   - How to identify potential leaders within an organization..48
   - Strategies for effectively developing and mentoring employees..50
7. **Conclusion** 52
   - Summary of key points... 53
   - Final thoughts on leadership....................................56
   - Resources for further learning 58

The Art of Leadership: Navigating the Path to Success

Introduction

"To handle yourself, use your head; to handle others, use your heart."

-Eleanor Roosevelt

The Art of Leadership: Navigating the Path to Success

The Definition of Leadership

Leadership is a complex and multifaceted concept that has been the subject of much study and discussion throughout history. At its core, leadership is the ability to guide and influence others towards a shared goal or vision. It is a process by which an individual or group is able to direct and motivate others to work towards a common objective.

There are many different definitions of leadership, each of which highlights different aspects of the concept. Some definitions emphasize the role of the leader as a visionary or a strategic thinker, while others focus on the leader's ability to inspire and motivate others. Still, others emphasize the leader's ability to make decisions and take action.

One commonly cited definition of leadership is that it is "the process of social influence in which one person can enlist the aid and support of others in the accomplishment of a common task". This definition highlights the leader's ability to influence and inspire others to work towards a shared goal.

The Art of Leadership: Navigating the Path to Success

Another definition of leadership is that it is "the ability to lead a group or organization towards the achievement of a common goal or vision." This definition emphasizes the leader's ability to guide and direct others towards a specific objective.

Leadership can also be seen as a combination of both trait-based and behavior-based characteristics. Trait-based leadership focuses on the inherent qualities of the leader such as confidence, intelligence, and integrity. On the other hand, behavior-based leadership focuses on the actions and decisions of the leader, such as how they communicate, delegate, and make decisions.

In conclusion, leadership is a complex and dynamic concept that can be defined in many different ways. It is a process by which an individual or group is able to direct and motivate others to work towards a common objective. A leader should have both trait and behavior-based characteristics, and should be able to guide, direct and inspire others to achieve a shared goal or vision.

The Importance of Leadership in Various Fields

Leadership is a vital component in virtually every field and industry. Whether it is in business, politics, education, or even sports, strong leaders are essential for achieving success and driving progress. In this chapter, we will explore the importance of leadership in various fields and how it can impact organizations, teams, and individuals.

In business, leadership is crucial for setting direction, making strategic decisions, and driving growth. Effective leaders in the business world are able to inspire and motivate their employees, create a positive and productive work environment, and make difficult decisions that drive the organization forward.

In politics, leadership is essential for leading a country, a community or a group. A strong leader in politics is able to inspire and mobilize people to work towards a common goal, and make difficult decisions that affect the lives of many. Additionally, they are often able to navigate complex political landscape, build and maintain alliances and negotiate to reach agreements.

The Art of Leadership: Navigating the Path to Success

In education, leadership is crucial for creating a positive and productive learning environment. Effective leaders in education are able to inspire and motivate students, create a culture of excellence, and make decisions that improve the quality of education. They also act as a role model for the students, staff and other educators.

In sports, leadership is vital for creating a winning team. Strong leaders in sports are able to inspire and motivate their teammates, make difficult decisions, and lead by example. Additionally, they are able to build a positive team culture and create a sense of unity among the team members.

In conclusion, leadership is an essential component in various fields and industries. Strong leaders are able to inspire and motivate others, make difficult decisions, and drive progress and success. Whether in business, politics, education, or sports, effective leadership is necessary for achieving goals and making a positive impact on individuals, teams, and organizations.

The Purpose of the Book

The purpose of this book is to provide readers with a comprehensive understanding of the principles and practices of leadership. The book is designed to help readers develop the skills and knowledge necessary to become effective leaders in their chosen field.

Throughout the book, readers will learn about the various traits and styles of leadership, and how to apply them in different situations. They will also learn about the importance of leading teams and organizations, and strategies for managing change and conflict. Additionally, the book will provide readers with insights on how to develop and mentor others, and how to identify potential leaders within an organization.

The book is intended for a wide audience, including individuals who are currently in leadership roles, those who aspire to become leaders in the future, and anyone else who wants to improve their leadership skills. It is suitable for both experienced leaders and those who are new to leadership roles.

The Art of Leadership: Navigating the Path to Success

This book is not meant to be a one-size-fits-all guide, but rather a comprehensive overview of leadership principles and practices. The readers are encouraged to apply the principles in their own unique way, taking into account the specific needs and circumstances of their organization.

The book also covers the most recent research and best practices in leadership, providing readers with the most up-to-date information. The goal is to give the readers a deeper understanding of leadership, and provide them with the tools they need to become successful leaders in their own right.

In conclusion, the purpose of this book is to provide readers with a comprehensive understanding of the principles and practices of leadership. It is designed to help readers develop the skills and knowledge necessary to become effective leaders in their chosen field.

The Traits of Effective Leaders

"Leaders must be close enough to relate to others, but far enough ahead to motivate them."

-John C. Maxwell

Characteristics and Qualities of Effective Leaders

Leadership is a complex and multifaceted concept, and effective leaders possess a wide range of characteristics and qualities that contribute to their success. In this chapter, we will explore some of the key characteristics and qualities that are commonly associated with effective leaders.

One of the most important characteristics of an effective leader is integrity. A leader with integrity is honest, ethical, and trustworthy. They are committed to doing what is right, even when it is difficult or unpopular. They also lead by example, and they walk the talk.

Another key characteristic of an effective leader is vision. A leader with vision is able to see the big picture and understand where the organization or team is headed. They have a clear sense of direction and are able to articulate a compelling vision that inspires others to work towards a common goal.

The Art of Leadership: Navigating the Path to Success

Effective leaders are also decisive. They are able to make difficult decisions, even when there is a lack of complete information. They are able to weigh the options and take the appropriate action, knowing that a good decision is better than no decision.

Effective leaders are also able to inspire and motivate others. They are able to create a sense of purpose and shared vision that inspires others to work towards a common goal. They are able to communicate this vision in a way that resonates with others, and they are able to inspire others to take action.

Effective leaders are also able to build and lead teams. They are able to create a positive and productive work environment, and they are able to build a sense of unity among team members. They are able to delegate effectively and empower others to take ownership of their work.

The Art of Leadership: Navigating the Path to Success

Effective leaders are also able to adapt to change. They are able to navigate through uncertainty, ambiguity, and rapid change. They are able to identify opportunities and threats, and they are able to make adjustments as needed.

In conclusion, effective leaders possess a wide range of characteristics and qualities that contribute to their success. These include integrity, vision, decisiveness, ability to inspire and motivate others, ability to build and lead teams and adaptability to change. While no leader possesses all of these qualities, being aware of these characteristics and striving to develop them is an important step towards becoming an effective leader.

Developing the Traits of Effective Leaders

While some individuals may possess natural leadership traits, it is important to note that leadership skills can be learned and developed over time. In this chapter, we will explore some strategies for developing the key traits of effective leaders.

Integrity: One of the most important traits of effective leaders is integrity. To develop integrity, it is important to practice honesty, ethics, and transparency in all interactions. Additionally, it is important to lead by example and to be consistent in words and actions.

Vision: To develop a visionary mindset, it is important to constantly look for new opportunities and to think creatively about the future. This can be achieved by reading widely, networking with other leaders, and seeking out new experiences. Additionally, it is important to be able to articulate a clear and compelling vision that inspires others.

Decisiveness: To develop the ability to make difficult decisions, it is important to practice effective problem-solving and decision-making skills. This can be achieved by gathering and analyzing information, considering multiple options, and weighing the pros and cons of each option. Additionally, it is important to be comfortable with uncertainty and to understand that a good decision is better than no decision.

Inspiration and Motivation: To develop the ability to inspire and motivate others, it is important to communicate effectively and to be able to connect with others on an emotional level. This can be achieved by practicing effective communication skills, understanding the needs and motivations of others, and being able to create a sense of shared purpose and vision.

Team Building: To develop the ability to build and lead teams, it is important to understand the dynamics of group behavior and to be able to create a positive and productive work environment. This can be achieved by developing effective communication and delegation skills, understanding the strengths and weaknesses of team members, and fostering a sense of collaboration and teamwork.

Adaptability: To develop the ability to adapt to change, it is important to be open to new ideas, to be willing to take risks, and to be comfortable with ambiguity. This can be achieved by seeking out new experiences, learning from failures, and being willing to make adjustments as needed.

In conclusion, while some individuals may possess natural leadership traits, it is important to note that leadership skills can be learned and developed over time. By practicing integrity, vision, decisiveness, inspiration and motivation, team building, and adaptability, individuals can develop the key traits of effective leaders. It takes time, effort and a consistent approach, but the rewards are worth it.

The Art of Leadership: Navigating the Path to Success

Examples of Leaders Who Possess the Traits of Effective Leaders

Throughout history, there have been many leaders who possess the key traits of effective leaders. In this chapter, we will explore some examples of leaders who possess integrity, vision, decisiveness, ability to inspire and motivate others, ability to build and lead teams, and adaptability to change.

One example of a leader who possessed integrity is Mahatma Gandhi. He was known for his honesty, ethics, and transparency, and he led by example. He also advocated for non-violent resistance and civil disobedience, which helped India achieve independence from British rule.

Another example of a leader with vision is Martin Luther King Jr. He had a clear sense of direction and was able to articulate a compelling vision that inspired others to work towards the Civil Rights Movement. His speeches and actions helped to mobilize the Civil Rights Movement in the United States and contributed to significant progress in the fight for racial equality.

The Art of Leadership: Navigating the Path to Success

An example of a leader who was decisive is Winston Churchill. He was able to make difficult decisions and take action during World War II, which ultimately led to the defeat of the Axis powers. Despite facing great challenges, Churchill remained steadfast in his determination to win the war and he inspired others to do the same.

An example of a leader who was able to inspire and motivate others is Nelson Mandela. He was able to create a sense of purpose and shared vision that inspired others to work towards the end of apartheid in South Africa. He also communicated this vision in a way that resonated with others and was able to inspire others to take action.

An example of a leader who was able to build and lead teams is Steve Jobs. He was able to create a positive and productive work environment, and he was able to build a sense of unity among team members. He also delegated effectively and empowered others to take ownership of their work which led to the success of Apple.

The Art of Leadership: Navigating the Path to Success

An example of a leader who was able to adapt to change is Mark Zuckerberg. He was able to navigate through uncertainty, ambiguity, and rapid change. He was able to identify opportunities and threats, and he was able to make adjustments as needed which led to the success of Facebook.

In conclusion, throughout history, there have been many leaders who possess the key traits of effective leaders. These examples of Mahatma Gandhi, Martin Luther King Jr, Winston Churchill, Nelson Mandela, Steve Jobs, and Mark Zuckerberg demonstrate the importance of integrity, vision, decisiveness, ability to inspire and motivate others, ability to build and lead teams, and adaptability to change in effective leadership. They are a source of inspiration for anyone who wants to develop leadership skills.

The Different Styles of Leadership

"Wisdom equals knowledge plus courage. You have to not only know what to do and when to do it, but you have to also be brave enough to follow through."

-Jarod Kintz

The Art of Leadership: Navigating the Path to Success

Overview of the Various Leadership Styles

Leadership is a complex and multifaceted concept, and there are many different styles of leadership that can be used in different situations. In this chapter, we will explore some of the most commonly used leadership styles and their characteristics.

Autocratic leadership is a style in which the leader makes all the decisions and gives orders without consulting others. It is often used in situations where quick decisions are needed, such as in a crisis. However, this style can be limiting as it does not allow for input or ideas from others, and it can lead to low morale and lack of motivation among team members.

Democratic leadership is a style in which the leader involves others in the decision-making process. This style is often used in situations where collaboration and input from others is needed. It promotes participation, ownership and commitment from the team members, and it can lead to higher morale and motivation.

The Art of Leadership: Navigating the Path to Success

Laissez-faire leadership is a style in which the leader provides little direction or guidance, allowing team members to make their own decisions. This style is often used in situations where the team members are highly skilled and motivated. However, it can also lead to confusion and lack of direction if the team members are not able to make effective decisions.

Transformational leadership is a style in which the leader inspires and motivates others to achieve a shared vision. This style is often used in situations where the leader is able to create a sense of purpose and shared vision that inspires and motivates others to take action.

Situational leadership is a style in which the leader adapts to the situation, and uses a combination of different styles of leadership depending on the situation. This style is often used when the leader is able to understand the specific needs and circumstances of the situation and adapts their leadership style accordingly.

The Art of Leadership: Navigating the Path to Success

Authentic leadership is a style in which the leader is transparent, honest, and ethical. They lead by example, and they walk the talk. They also prioritize the well-being and development of their team members.

In conclusion, there are many different styles of leadership that can be used in different situations. Each style has its own strengths and weaknesses, and it's important for leaders to understand the different styles and know when to use them effectively. It's also important for leaders to be flexible and adapt their leadership style as the situation changes. The key is to be aware of the different leadership styles and to be able to use them effectively in different situations.

Advantages and Disadvantages of Various Leadership Styles

Different leadership styles have their own advantages and disadvantages, and it's important for leaders to understand the pros and cons of each style in order to use them effectively. In this chapter, we will explore the advantages and disadvantages of the most commonly used leadership styles.

Autocratic leadership has the advantage of allowing for quick decision-making and efficient problem-solving. This style is often used in situations where quick decisions are needed, such as in a crisis. However, the disadvantage of this style is that it does not allow for input or ideas from others, which can lead to low morale, lack of motivation, and lack of creativity among team members.

Democratic leadership has the advantage of involving others in the decision-making process. This style promotes participation, ownership, and commitment from the team members, and it can lead to higher morale and motivation. However, the disadvantage of this style is that it can be time-consuming and can lead to slow decision-making.

The Art of Leadership: Navigating the Path to Success

Laissez-faire leadership has the advantage of allowing team members to make their own decisions and take ownership of their work. This style is often used in situations where the team members are highly skilled and motivated. However, the disadvantage of this style is that it can lead to confusion, lack of direction, and lack of accountability if the team members are not able to make effective decisions.

Transformational leadership has the advantage of inspiring and motivating others to achieve a shared vision. This style can lead to high levels of commitment, motivation, and creativity among team members. However, it can be difficult to implement and maintain, especially if the leader is not able to create a strong sense of purpose and shared vision.

Situational leadership has the advantage of adapting to the situation, which allows leaders to use different styles depending on the needs of the team and the situation. This style can be very effective in dynamic environments, but it requires a high level of situational awareness and flexibility from the leader.

The Art of Leadership: Navigating the Path to Success

Authentic leadership has the advantage of promoting transparency, honesty, and ethics, which can lead to trust and credibility among team members and stakeholders. However, it can be difficult to maintain authenticity in all situations, and it requires a high level of self-awareness and self-regulation from the leader.

In conclusion, each leadership style has its own advantages and disadvantages, and it's important for leaders to understand the pros and cons of each style in order to use them effectively. It's also important for leaders to be flexible and adapt their leadership style as the situation changes.

The Art of Leadership: Navigating the Path to Success

How to Determine the Best Leadership Style for a Given Situation

As we have seen in the previous chapter, different leadership styles have their own advantages and disadvantages, and it's important for leaders to understand the pros and cons of each style in order to use them effectively. In this chapter, we will explore how to determine the best leadership style for a given situation.

The first step in determining the best leadership style for a given situation is to understand the situation itself. This includes understanding the goals and objectives of the team or organization, the strengths and weaknesses of the team members, and the external factors that may be impacting the situation.

Once you have a clear understanding of the situation, you can then evaluate the different leadership styles and determine which one is best suited for the situation. For example, if the situation requires quick decision-making and efficient problem-solving, then an autocratic leadership style may be the best choice.

The Art of Leadership: Navigating the Path to Success

If the situation requires collaboration and input from others, then a democratic leadership style may be the best choice. It's also important to consider the team members and their individual needs and preferences. For example, some team members may prefer a more hands-off approach and may respond well to a laissez-faire leadership style, while others may prefer a more hands-on approach and may respond well to a transformational leadership style.

Another important aspect to consider is the level of development of the team members. For example, team members who are less experienced may require a more directive leadership style, while team members who are more experienced may require a more delegative or laissez-faire leadership style.

In conclusion, determining the best leadership style for a given situation requires a thorough understanding of the situation, the team members, and their individual needs and preferences. It's important for leaders to be able to evaluate different leadership styles and determine which one is best suited for the situation. It's also important for leaders to be flexible and adapt their leadership style as the situation changes.

Leading Teams and Organizations

"The ultimate measure of a man is not where he stands in moments of comfort, but where he stands at times of challenge and controversy."

-Martin Luther King, Jr.

The Role of the Leader in Building and Leading Teams

Leadership is not only about making decisions and giving orders, it's also about building and leading teams. In this chapter, we will explore the role of the leader in building and leading teams.

The first step in building a team is to establish a clear vision and a set of goals for the team to work towards. The leader should clearly communicate the vision and goals to the team members and ensure that everyone is on the same page.

Once the vision and goals are established, the leader should work to build a strong and cohesive team. This includes selecting the right team members, fostering a positive and inclusive team culture, and encouraging collaboration and communication among team members.

A leader should also play an active role in developing the skills and abilities of the team members. This includes providing training and development opportunities and giving team members the autonomy to take on new challenges and responsibilities.

The Art of Leadership: Navigating the Path to Success

In leading the team, a leader should set clear expectations and hold team members accountable for their performance. They should also provide regular feedback and recognition for a job well done. A leader should also lead by example, and be a role model for the team.

In addition to this, a leader should also be able to manage conflicts within the team and to be able to resolve them in a timely and effective manner. They should also be able to build trust and credibility among team members and stakeholders.

In conclusion, the role of the leader in building and leading teams is crucial for the success of the team. A leader should be able to establish a clear vision and set of goals, build a strong and cohesive team, develop the skills and abilities of the team members, lead by example, and manage conflicts within the team. The leader should also be able to build trust and credibility among team members and stakeholders.

How to Create a Positive and Productive Work Environment

A positive and productive work environment is essential for the success of any team or organization. In this chapter, we will explore how to create a positive and productive work environment.

One of the most important aspects of creating a positive and productive work environment is fostering a culture of trust and respect. This includes treating all team members with dignity and respect, encouraging open communication, and promoting a sense of teamwork and collaboration. Another important aspect is to provide opportunities for professional development and growth. This can include providing training and development opportunities, as well as opportunities for team members to take on new challenges and responsibilities. This can also include fostering a culture of innovation and experimentation, encouraging team members to come up with new ideas and take calculated risks.

The Art of Leadership: Navigating the Path to Success

It's also important to recognize and reward the achievements of team members. This can include providing regular feedback, as well as tangible rewards such as bonuses or promotions. Recognition and rewards can help to boost morale and motivation among team members. Creating a positive and productive work environment also means providing support and resources to team members. This can include providing the necessary equipment and technology, as well as providing access to resources such as mental health support, or other employee assistance programs.

In addition to this, a leader should also be able to manage conflicts within the team and to be able to resolve them in a timely and effective manner. They should also be able to build trust and credibility among team members and stakeholders.

In conclusion, creating a positive and productive work environment requires a combination of different strategies. It's important to foster a culture of trust and respect, provide opportunities for professional development and growth, recognize and reward the achievements of team members, and provide support and resources to team members.

The Art of Leadership: Navigating the Path to Success

Additionally, a leader should be able to manage conflicts within the team and to be able to resolve them in a timely and effective manner. They should also be able to build trust and credibility among team members and stakeholders.

Strategies for Effective Communication and Delegation

Effective communication and delegation are crucial for the success of any team or organization. In this chapter, we will explore strategies for effective communication and delegation.

Effective communication is essential for building trust and fostering collaboration among team members. One strategy for effective communication is to be clear and concise when communicating goals, expectations, and instructions. This can include using simple language, providing visual aids, and repeating important information to ensure that it is understood.

Another strategy for effective communication is to actively listen to the perspectives and opinions of others. This can include asking questions, providing feedback, and encouraging open and honest dialogue. In addition, it's important to be aware of different communication styles and to adapt accordingly.

The Art of Leadership: Navigating the Path to Success

Effective delegation is also important for building a strong and productive team. One strategy for effective delegation is to clearly define the tasks and responsibilities that are being delegated, as well as the expected outcomes. This can include providing detailed instructions, setting clear deadlines and providing necessary resources and support. Another strategy for effective delegation is to identify the right person for the task, match the task with their skills and abilities. Also, it's important to provide team members with the proper training, tools, and guidance they need to complete their tasks. Additionally, it's important to set clear expectations for communication during the delegation process, such as regular check-ins and progress updates. It's also important to monitor the progress of delegated tasks and to provide feedback and recognition for a job well done. This can include regular check-ins, progress reports, and providing constructive feedback.

In conclusion, effective communication and delegation are crucial for the success of any team or organization. Strategies for effective communication include being clear and concise, actively listening to the perspectives and opinions of others, and adapting to different communication styles. Strategies for effective delegation include clearly

The Art of Leadership: Navigating the Path to Success

defining tasks and responsibilities, matching tasks with team members' skills and abilities, and providing proper training, tools, and guidance. Additionally, effective delegation includes setting clear expectations for communication during the delegation process, monitoring progress and providing feedback and recognition for a job well done.

The Art of Leadership: Navigating the Path to Success

Managing Change and Conflict

"My job is not to be easy on people. My job is to take these great people we have and to push them and make them even better."

-Steve Jobs

The Leader's Role in Managing Change and Conflict

Change and conflict are inevitable in any organization, and the leader plays a critical role in managing both. In this chapter, we will explore the leader's role in managing change and conflict.

Managing change is an ongoing process, and leaders must be able to anticipate, plan for, and respond to change. One strategy for managing change is to clearly communicate the reasons for the change and the expected outcomes to all stakeholders. This can include providing regular updates and involving team members in the planning and implementation process.

Another strategy for managing change is to build buy-in and support among team members. This can include involving team members in the planning and implementation process, providing training and development opportunities, and recognizing and rewarding team members for their efforts.

The Art of Leadership: Navigating the Path to Success

Managing conflict is also an important aspect of leadership. One strategy for managing conflict is to actively listen to all perspectives and to encourage open and honest dialogue. This can include providing a safe space for team members to express their concerns and to offer solutions. Another strategy for managing conflict is to identify the underlying issues and to focus on finding a solution that addresses the concerns of all parties involved. This can include involving a neutral third party, such as a mediator, to help facilitate the process.

In conclusion, the leader's role in managing change and conflict is crucial for the success of any team or organization. Strategies for managing change include clearly communicating the reasons for the change, building buy-in and support among team members, and involving team members in the planning and implementation process. Strategies for managing conflict include actively listening to all perspectives, identifying the underlying issues, and finding a solution that addresses the concerns of all parties involved. The leader should also be able to involve a neutral third party, such as a mediator, to help facilitate the process.

Strategies for Effectively Navigating Resistance to Change

Change is an inevitable part of any organization, but it's not always easy to implement. Resistance to change is a common obstacle that leaders must navigate. In this chapter, we will explore strategies for effectively navigating resistance to change.

One strategy for effectively navigating resistance to change is to communicate the reasons for the change and the expected outcomes clearly and consistently to all stakeholders. This can include providing regular updates and involving team members in the planning and implementation process. By involving team members in the planning process, they will feel more invested in the change and will be more likely to support it.

Another strategy is to address the concerns and fears of those who may be resistant to change. This can include identifying the underlying issues that are causing resistance, and addressing them directly. It can also include providing training and development opportunities to help team members develop the skills they need to adapt to the change. Another strategy is to build a coalition of support among key stakeholders. This can include identifying individuals or groups who are likely to support the change, and working with them to build a coalition that can help to overcome resistance.

It's also important to be patient and persistent when implementing change. Change takes time, and it's not always easy to overcome resistance. It's important to remain consistent and persistent in communicating the reasons for the change, addressing concerns, and building support.

In conclusion, resistance to change is a common obstacle that leaders must navigate. Strategies for effectively navigating resistance include communicating the reasons for the change clearly, addressing concerns and fears of those who may be resistant, building a coalition of support among key stakeholders, and being patient and persistent in implementing the change. It's important to involve team members in the planning process, address underlying issues, provide training and development opportunities and build support among key stakeholders.

Techniques for Resolving Conflicts and Promoting Collaboration

Conflict resolution and collaboration are crucial for the success of any team or organization. In this chapter, we will explore techniques for resolving conflicts and promoting collaboration.

One technique for resolving conflicts is to encourage active listening and open communication. This can include creating a safe space for team members to express their concerns, and encouraging open and honest dialogue. This can also include asking questions, providing feedback, and actively listening to the perspectives and opinions of others. Another technique for resolving conflicts is to identify the underlying issues and to focus on finding a solution that addresses the concerns of all parties involved. This can include involving a neutral third party, such as a mediator, to help facilitate the process.

Promoting collaboration is also an important aspect of leadership. One technique for promoting collaboration is to foster a culture of trust and respect. This can include treating all team members with dignity and respect, encouraging open communication, and promoting a sense of teamwork and collaboration.

Another technique for promoting collaboration is to provide opportunities for team members to work together on shared goals and objectives. This can include creating cross-functional teams, encouraging brainstorming and idea-sharing, and recognizing and rewarding team members for their contributions.

In conclusion, resolving conflicts and promoting collaboration are crucial for the success of any team or organization. Techniques for resolving conflicts include encouraging active listening and open communication, identifying underlying issues, and involving a neutral third party. Techniques for promoting collaboration include fostering a culture of trust and respect, providing opportunities for team members to work together, and recognizing and rewarding team members for their contributions.

Developing and Mentoring Others

"If your actions inspire others to dream more, learn more, do more and become more, you are a leader."

-John Quincy Adams

The Importance of Developing and Mentoring Others

Developing and mentoring others is a critical aspect of leadership. In this chapter, we will explore the importance of developing and mentoring others.

One important aspect of developing and mentoring others is to provide opportunities for professional development and growth. This can include providing training and development opportunities, as well as opportunities for team members to take on new challenges and responsibilities. This not only helps to improve the skills and abilities of team members, but also helps to prepare them for leadership roles in the future.

Another important aspect of developing and mentoring others is to provide guidance and support. This can include providing feedback, answering questions, and offering advice and mentorship. A good mentor should be a role model, and should be able to share their experience and knowledge with others.

Developing and mentoring others also helps to build a more diverse and inclusive workforce. By providing opportunities for professional development, it allows individuals from different backgrounds and experiences to rise to leadership roles, leading to a more diverse and inclusive workforce.

In addition, mentoring and development can also have a positive impact on employee engagement, motivation and job satisfaction. When employees are provided with the opportunity to learn and grow, they are more likely to feel valued and engaged in their work.

In conclusion, developing and mentoring others is a critical aspect of leadership. It helps to provide opportunities for professional development and growth, guidance, and support, as well as building a more diverse and inclusive workforce. It also has a positive impact on employee engagement, motivation and job satisfaction. A good leader should be able to recognize the potential of others, and to provide the opportunities and guidance to help them reach their full potential.

The Art of Leadership: Navigating the Path to Success

How to Identify Potential Leaders within an Organization

Identifying potential leaders within an organization is an important aspect of building a strong and effective leadership team. In this chapter, we will explore how to identify potential leaders within an organization.

One way to identify potential leaders is to look for individuals who demonstrate initiative and take on leadership roles in their current positions. These individuals are often proactive, and they are not afraid to step up and take charge when necessary. They also tend to be effective problem-solvers and decision-makers.

Another way to identify potential leaders is to look for individuals who are well-respected by their peers and colleagues. These individuals often have strong communication and interpersonal skills, and they are able to build trust and credibility among their team members.
It's also important to look for individuals who are open to learning and development. Potential leaders are often eager to learn new skills and take on new challenges. They are also able to adapt to change and are willing to take calculated risks.

The Art of Leadership: Navigating the Path to Success

Another way to identify potential leaders is to look for individuals who have a strong understanding of the organization's mission, values, and goals. These individuals are often able to align their own goals with those of the organization, and they are committed to achieving them.

In conclusion, identifying potential leaders within an organization requires a combination of different strategies. It's important to look for individuals who demonstrate initiative, are well-respected by their peers and colleagues, open to learning and development, and have a strong understanding of the organization's mission, values, and goals. Additionally, a leader should be able to identify potential leaders by evaluating their skills, abilities, and performance, as well as their potential for growth and development within the organization.

Strategies for Effectively Developing and Mentoring Employees

Effectively developing and mentoring employees is a critical aspect of leadership. In this chapter, we will explore strategies for effectively developing and mentoring employees.

One strategy for effectively developing and mentoring employees is to provide regular feedback and coaching. This can include providing regular performance evaluations, setting clear goals and expectations, and providing constructive feedback on areas for improvement.

Another strategy is to provide opportunities for professional development and growth. This can include providing training and development opportunities, such as workshops, seminars, and mentoring programs. It can also include offering opportunities for team members to take on new challenges and responsibilities, such as leading a project or team.

Another strategy is to build a mentoring culture in the organization. This can include encouraging experienced employees to mentor and coach newer employees, and recognizing and rewarding those who do. This can create a positive cycle of mentoring and development, and can help to build a strong and effective leadership team.

In addition, it's important to create an environment that fosters learning and development. This can include providing access to relevant resources such as books, articles, and webinars, as well as promoting a culture of continuous learning.

In conclusion, effectively developing and mentoring employees is a critical aspect of leadership. Strategies for effectively developing and mentoring employees include providing regular feedback and coaching, providing opportunities for professional development and growth, building a mentoring culture in the organization, and creating an environment that fosters learning and development. A good leader should be able to recognize the potential of their employees, and provide them with the opportunities and guidance they need to reach their full potential.

Conclusion

"Customers will never love a company until employees love it first."

- Simon Sinek

Key Points

In this book, we have covered a wide range of topics related to leadership, including the definition of leadership, the importance of leadership in various fields, the characteristics and qualities of effective leaders, the various leadership styles, and strategies for effective communication and delegation. We also discussed the leader's role in building and leading teams, creating a positive and productive work environment, managing change and conflict, and developing and mentoring others.

Here are some of the key points to remember from this book:

1. Leadership is the ability to inspire and guide others towards a shared goal or vision.

2. Leadership is important in all fields, including business, government, education, and non-profit organizations.

3. Effective leaders possess a combination of characteristics and qualities such as integrity, honesty, empathy, and the ability to inspire and motivate others.

The Art of Leadership: Navigating the Path to Success

4. Different situations may require different leadership styles, and it's important for leaders to be able to adapt to different situations.

5. Effective communication and delegation are crucial for building a strong and productive team.

6. The leader plays a critical role in creating a positive and productive work environment.

7. Change and conflict are inevitable in any organization, and leaders must be able to anticipate, plan for, and respond to change.

8. Developing and mentoring others is a critical aspect of leadership and is important for building a strong and effective leadership team.

9. Identifying potential leaders within an organization is an important aspect of building a strong and effective leadership team.

10. Strategies for effectively developing and mentoring employees include providing regular feedback and coaching, providing opportunities for professional development and growth, building a mentoring culture in the organization, and creating an environment that fosters learning and development.

This book has provided an overview of the key concepts and strategies related to leadership. It's important to remember that leadership is a continuous learning process and it's important for leaders to continue to develop their skills and abilities over time.

Final Thoughts on Leadership

Throughout this book, we have explored various aspects of leadership and the importance of leadership in different fields. From defining leadership, to discussing the characteristics and qualities of effective leaders, to exploring strategies for effective communication and delegation, we have covered a wide range of topics.

Leadership is a complex and ever-evolving concept, and there is no single formula for success. Every leader is unique, and the most effective leaders are those who are able to adapt their leadership style to the specific needs of their organization and team.

It's also important to remember that leadership is not just about the leader, but also about the team and the organization as a whole. A good leader should be able to create a positive and productive work environment, build and lead effective teams, and develop and mentor others. Moreover, effective leadership requires continuous learning and development. Leaders must be willing to adapt to new challenges and changes, and to continuously improve their skills and abilities.

The Art of Leadership: Navigating the Path to Success

In conclusion, leadership is an essential aspect of any organization, and effective leaders are critical for the success of any team or organization. The leader's role is to inspire and guide others towards a shared goal or vision, and to create a positive and productive work environment. A good leader should be able to adapt to different situations, be a continuous learner, and have the ability to develop and mentor others.

Resources for Further Learning

Leadership is a complex and ever-evolving concept, and there is always more to learn and discover. In this chapter, we will provide a list of resources for further learning on leadership.

1. Books: There are many books available on leadership, covering a wide range of topics. Some popular books on leadership include "The Art of War" by Sun Tzu, "The 7 Habits of Highly Effective People" by Stephen Covey, "Leadership: The Power of Emotional Intelligence" by Daniel Goleman, and "Good to Great: Why Some Companies Make the Leap and Others Don't" by Jim Collins.

2. Online Courses: Many universities and organizations offer online courses on leadership, which can be a great way to learn more about leadership in a structured and convenient way. Some popular online course providers include Coursera, Udemy, and LinkedIn Learning.

3. Conferences and Workshops: Conferences and workshops on leadership can be a great way to learn from experts in the field and network with other leaders. Some popular conferences on leadership include the World Leadership Forum, the Harvard Business Review Leadership Summit, and the Leadership Summit.

4. Professional Organizations: Joining a professional organization related to leadership can be a great way to learn more about leadership and network with other leaders. Some popular professional organizations include the International Leadership Association, the American Leadership Forum, and the Institute of Leadership and Management.

5. Leadership Blogs and Podcasts: There are many blogs and podcasts available that cover leadership topics, and can be a great way to learn more about leadership in your spare time. Some popular blogs and podcasts include the Harvard Business Review Leadership Blog, the Leadership Freak Podcast, and the Inc. Leadership Blog.

The Art of Leadership: Navigating the Path to Success

In conclusion, there are many resources available for further learning on leadership. From books, to online courses, to conferences and workshops, to professional organizations, to blogs and podcasts, there is always more to learn and discover about leadership. A good leader should always be looking for ways to improve their skills and abilities and be a continuous learner.

www.ingramcontent.com/pod-product-compliance
Lightning Source LLC
Chambersburg PA
CBHW050310220526
45465CB00005B/1926